East Runton Lower Common, early in the 20th century

Introduction

The concept of East and West Runton as separate entities rather than as two halves of one community is of relatively recent origin. It has certainly developed greatly since World War 2 with the expansion of both villages and was probably increased by the closure in 1958 of the school at East Runton, which had been a focal point of activity in the parish for over 100 years. Until well into the 19th century official references were simply to Runton, or to variant forms such as Runcton, Ronton or Rungeton. Confusion has frequently arisen with Roughton or, the Runctons of north-west Norfolk. A further complication is that Runton was closely linked with its neighbour Beeston from a very early date. In the Domesday Book Runton church and its lands are included in the measurement of Beeston. References to Runton have therefore to be sought also under Beeston, and to some extent vice versa.

It will probably never be possible to write a comprehensive and coherent story of Runton: parish registers of baptisms, marriages and burials which should normally commence in 1558, if not in 1538, date only from the 1740s, while the accounts of churchwardens and overseers of the poor are also missing. Much interesting material is, however, to be found in the records, mainly court rolls and books, of the principal manors holding land here – Beeston-iuxta-Mare (later Regis), Beeston Priory, Runton Felbrigg's, Runton Hayes and Runton Stubbes. Information has to be gathered from various different sources in the hope that some relationship may be found. So, instead of a connected story, a series of odd glimpses of some former inhabitants is presented in this booklet.

G. F. Leake

Before Domesday

What evidence there is for human activity in Runton before 1086 results mainly from random surface finds of worked flints or sherds of pottery. While there has been no large-scale field-walking and much of the land is now permanently under grass, scatters of Mesolithic and Neolithic tools have been found in the fields between the two villages. Several Palaeolithic hand-axes have also been discovered, but the once well-known eoliths are now generally considered to be flints shaped by natural processes.

It is interesting to note that there seems to be a concentration of finds of artefacts in the vicinity of Woman Hithe at West Runton. From the cliff-face came a barrel-shaped pottery vessel of the Bronze Age and a bowl of Rinyo-Clacton grooved ware dating from the Neolithic period, together with two skeletons and pottery of the Iron Age, Romano-British and Medieval periods. A few Roman coins and a gold stater have also been discovered there. This obviously reflects much early activity at a favoured site, but the number of finds may be related to the intensity of wear on the sandy soil of the car park and its surroundings in recent years. From East Runton come two jet rings about 2½ inches (63 mm) in diameter, described as pendants dating from the Romano-British period.

New defences (see page 40), looking east from West Runton gap (Woman Hithe).
The elephant (see page 38) was found in this section.

In 1859 a brief and vague account was given of the digging-up of 'several rude black urns filled with burnt bones' from a ploughed field somewhere in Runton. The site and fate of the urns are now unknown.

The presence of iron slag near the so-called Roman Camp has been known for at least two centuries. In 1883 the site and the surrounding pits known as Hills and Holes were surveyed and slag was found as a component of the earthwork. Yet the idea persisted that the pits had been made for human habitation. Excavation by Dr R. F. Tylecote in 1964 showed that these were in fact dug to provide the nodules of iron oxide used in a nearby smelting furnace, which could have produced some 50 tons of metal from about 1,000 pits. The period during which the bloomery site operated was probably some time between AD 850 and 1150.

Early manorial situation

The story is not at all clear from the late 11th to the early 13th century, despite gradually increasing documentation. It is concerned mainly with the break-up and the re-assembly of manors and the creation of new ones, and the details remain obscure.

The currently accepted view is that in Beeston (Besentuna) two Norman magnates, Hugh de Montfort and William d'Ecouis, each held one ploughland (taken to be about 120 acres, or 50 hectares): and that in Runton (Runetune) d'Ecouis held another ploughland, while Roger Bigod, Sheriff of Norfolk and Suffolk, had 30 acres. This view ignores the identification by Blomefield in his *Topographical History &c of the County of Norfolk*, vol. V, 1775, of another of de Montfort's holdings, one ploughland in Rugutune, as being at Runton. The *Victoria County History of Norfolk*, vol. 2, 1906, and subsequent publications, take this to be Roughton.

However, Blomefield's view should be borne in mind, since if correct it would make for an easier understanding of the manorial situation in the 13th century. In 1207 and 1209 Hubert de Burgh, the defender of Dover, later justiciar and Earl of Kent, purchased from a group of people their various parts of two knight's fees in Beeston and Runton. Whether or not Hubert himself already held some part of Beeston and Runton is not clear, but during his troubled relationship with Henry III the Beeston manor, in which Runton was subsumed, was stated to be 'of his inheritance'. He granted the manor to one of his supporters, Sir Philip Basset, a grant confirmed in 1243 by his son John. Basset is stated to have held the two knight's fees in Beeston and Runton as of the Honour of Haughley. This Honour (a term loosely defined as a grouping of several knight's fees, lordships and manors under one administration) had been created for Hugh de Montfort and was connected with the Constableship of Dover Castle which he held. Once more confusion sets in, for Hubert de Burgh similarly held Dover Castle and was granted the Honour of Haughley before 1219. When the Beeston manor came to Robert De Vere, 5th Earl of Oxford, and Alice his wife, and so to their grandson, John de Warenne, it was still stated to be held of Haughley, and as in Basset's time paid 20 shillings (£1) castle guard annually to Dover Castle.

While Hubert de Burgh re-assembled an estate that had been broken up, the other major holding in Beeston and Runton became fragmented. The estate of William d'Ecouis apparently came to Gilbert de Norfolk who died, probably around the turn of the 12th century, leaving only five daughters. The manor or manors and the advowson of Runton church appear to have been divided between them so that when deeds conveying lands in Runton or Beeston refer to one-fifth of a property it seems likely that they stem from this source.

It is generally accepted that Beeston Priory was founded about 1216 by Margaret de Cressy and that further benefactions were made by her daughter-in-law, Isabella. Indeed, the latter has also been considered to be the foundress. However, other gifts were made to the Priory after her death in 1263. For example, in December 1279 Margaret, widow of Nicholas de Chostes, made a quitclaim to the Prior and Convent of Beeston renouncing her dower rights in the lands and manorial privileges which her husband had formerly possessed, including one-fifth of the advowson of Runton church.

It may be that the outcome of these reorganisations made in the 13th century is represented approximately by the way in which the profits of 'wreck of sea', i.e. flotsam and jetsam, coming ashore anywhere at Beeston or Runton were shared between the various manors 100 years later: 'The lord of Beeston has one half, and of the other half the Prior of Beeston has 3 parts, the lord of Felbrigg has 1½ parts and John de Plumstede has ½ part' from which it is clear that each 'part' is one-fifth of the second half of the profits.

This would account for four of the five main manors in Runton; Beeston-iuxta-Mare (later Regis); Beeston Priory; Runton Felbrigg's; and that which became Runton Stubbes. Regarding the fifth one, in 1275 the jurors of the court of the Hundred of North Erpingham were unable to say by what right John Haye claimed manorial privileges here, but the existing court rolls of the manor of Runton Hayes are earlier than any of the others, beginning in 1281, so his case must have been well founded.

Coastal affairs

One thread runs throughout the history of Runton up to the present day: the continual ravaging of the land by the sea. Professor K. Clayton has been quoted as saying that the coastline between Weybourne and Happisburgh has been retreating at a rate of about one metre a year for 6,000 years. This may not be entirely true of Runton, for some fields which were already suffering erosion in the later 15th century had not yet finally disappeared in 1840 when the tithe map was drawn.

It should, however, come as no surprise to learn that Runton has lost a settlement just as Shipden off Cromer was lost, although over a longer period of time. In the late 15th century in East Runton there were 11 messuages, four 'howses' and two granges situated either in Seagate, as Beach Road was then called, or slightly to the west 'by the Sea's Syde'. The tithe map of 1840 shows that there were still six cottages and a wash-house on the cliff-top. An etching by Robert Blake in 1834 shows that some of these buildings were thatched. By the time of the survey made in 1885 for the first edition of the six-inch Ordnance Survey map all had gone. Another had been built about 100 yards west of the Gap. This, known as Strongarm's Cottage from the nickname of its occupant, also disappeared soon after World War 1.

West Runton does not appear to have had any similar settlement. In the late 15th century there were only arable strips beyond the King's meadows at the end of 'Medowe Lane', as Water Lane was then called. It may be to West Runton that Edmund Hooke referred in his bequest, in 1773/4, setting up a charity to provide 'fewel for the poor of Beeston and Upper Runton'.

While a survey of the 1490s refers to several pieces of land as having been

East Runton gap in the 1890s

Towards West Runton, autumn 2005. Just how much land at the bottom of the picture has been removed by the 'pounding of the waves' since medieval times?

reduced in size through erosion, the court rolls of the manor of Runton Stubbes illustrate what must have occurred very often. In 1539 Isabella Smythe inherited from her father, Robert Burflete, a cottage and 2½ acres of land. Robert Macke, son of her second marriage, was six years old when the property came to him in 1560, and he was therefore made the ward of his grandmother, Isabell Hillington. In 1564, on his behalf, she sought permission 'to take down, overthrow and draw back a house or cottage because the ebb and flow of the water would prevent it being rebuilt if it were not to be destroyed by the pounding of the waves'. As she paid 40 pence, quite a large sum, for the privilege one must suppose that the building was dismantled and re-erected further inland. Yet, in 1617, after Robert Macke's death had been reported, a marginal note in the court book stated 'the howse and all the land is in the sea saving V roods' (i.e., except for 1¼ acres, or half a hectare).

'Wreck of sea' was a valued perquisite. In December 1392, at a court of the manor of Beeston-iuxta-Mare, the jurors of East Runton reported that the following had come ashore: '40 barrels, 20 empty, 20 full of beer; 46 planks of oak panelling; one oak tree, part of a ship called "le Dele"; one windlass, four spars and two steering oars'. The Beeston jurors also reported the finding of '9 planks of oak panelling; 30 wooden stakes and a small barrel'. A month later the court of Runton Felbrigg's manor met, and referred to what may well have been the same wreck, with the finding of an unspecified number of barrels of beer and '36 boards of oak panelling'. The proceeds were to be divided according to the formula already mentioned.

A diplomatic incident between England and Scotland was caused on 2nd January 1588/9, when a Scottish ship, the *Esperance*, returning home from France was wrecked at Runton and its cargo allegedly looted by Roger Windham of Felbrigg and others. Representations were made by the Scottish king to Queen Elizabeth and on 22nd January 1588/9 the Privy Council ordered the Deputy Lieutenants of the county to inquire into the matter. One of these men, Sir Edward Clere, was regarded by Windham as his bitter enemy and was the only one to sign the report. As a result of their findings Windham was committed to the Marshalsea prison in London.

A different commission was set up on 25th August 1589 at Sheringham and reported more favourably. It appeared that a crowd of 200 or more, including Roger Windham, had gathered on the shore and was offered half the value of merchandise saved. Many people accepted the offer and took the rescued goods to Runton parsonage which was unoccupied at the time. Roger prevented some looting, but much took place by known and unknown persons. Next day his brother, Sir Francis Windham, a justice of Common Pleas, ensured that the remaining merchandise was salvaged by his staff and was stored at his various houses and in Beeston rectory. He issued search warrants to the constables of neighbouring villages for the recovery of the loot, but much remained missing. The keys to the various houses concerned were handed to the Scottish merchants. By 10th August 1590 the Privy Council reported that Windham had been cleared of the charges but was again committed to the Marshalsea until he had satisfied the Scots. Finally, on 28th July 1591, as the latter refused to prosecute, he was ordered to pay them £200 and to assist the Judge of the Admiralty in his inquiries.

Flint nodules and battered sea defences

Many present inhabitants of Runton will recall ships coming ashore in gales or fog, although with modern navigational aids

The Gold Crown *ashore at East Runton, with Cromer lifeboat and a tug in attendance, November 1933.*

this is almost a thing of the past. On the night of 20th November 1933, in dense fog, the motor barge *Gold Crown*, laden with dust coal for Norwich power station, went aground at Wood Point, East Runton, and was not refloated until nine days later. Part of the cargo was jettisoned and many people obtained a good supply of free coal, though not without hard work.

The Lady Gwynfred *beached at East Runton, November 1936*

On 18th November 1936, the sailing barge *Lady Gwynfred*, came ashore near Wood Point, but was eventually refloated. On 12th November 1937 the *Hibernia* was less fortunate and broke up on East Runton beach.

Cliff falls and slips continue to gnaw away at the coastline. It is probably over 30 years since Wood Point itself, a low promontory of chalk and clay protruding about 20 feet (six metres) onto the beach, was finally eroded. In Savin's *History of Cromer*, 1936, mention is made of a large glacial boulder, then about 100 yards from the cliff at Goss's Gap. This was reputed to have been at the foot of the cliff in the early 19th century. The inscription it bears, though greatly battered, consists of the initials SC and a date which appears to be 1773. This stone is now seldom visible except at Spring tides.

Finally, mention must be made of the disastrous tidal surge which occurred on the night of 31st January 1953. Contrary to a recent account, East Runton was not flooded, but much damage was caused along the shore, to the cliffs, the sea wall and the public lavatories. Beach huts were smashed and carried away by the violence of the sea and wind. But the boats had all been pulled up the gangway to safety before the waters reached their full height, when the run of the waves was nearly halfway up the slope and spray came over the cliff top.

Half-Year Lands

As a consequence of the Commons Registration Act, 1965, a costly enquiry was held in November 1975 and January 1976 to determine what was common land and what rights were connected with it and what grazing rights existed over the half-year lands. These latter were a carry-over from medieval communal agriculture, where after harvest the unsown arable land lay open for controlled grazing from Michaelmas to Lady Day. There has been no Enclosure Act for Runton and both the tithe map of 1840 and the first six-inch Ordnance Survey map of 1885 reveal considerable evidence of an open-field parish, with many narrow strips of land, some of less than a quarter of an acre, divided only by grass balks. It was principally this area lying outside the core of the two villages, and by now mostly enclosed or amalgamated into larger fields, over which half-year rights were claimed on behalf of the inhabitants of Runton.

In the event, the Commissioner registered all the existing commons, which

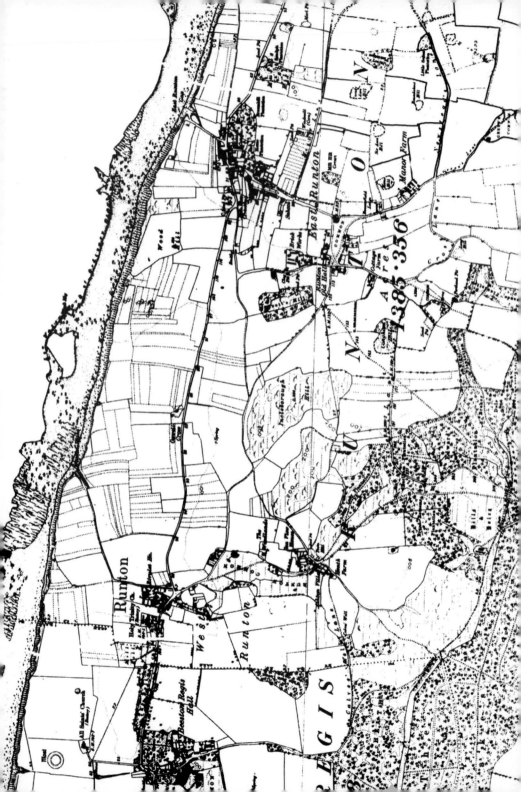

meant that three small ones shown on the tithe map, at Deer's Hill and on either side of the road at Oxwell Cross, had been finally lost. He refused to confirm any rights over the commons or over the former half-year lands. Regarding the latter, he remarked that the claimed rights had acted as 'a restrictive covenant against the use of half-year land for purposes inconsistent with grazing'. So ended a controversy that had continued on-and-off since the end of the 19th century at least, and had been marked by the deep and sincere conviction of the claimants in their rights as part of an ancient heritage.

Situated on the northern face of the Cromer–Holt Ridge and its adjoining coastal plain, Runton lies in that part of Norfolk where an integrated sheep–corn husbandry was practised during the Middle Ages and long afterwards. The fertility of sandy soil was maintained by the dung of sheep which were folded on fallow land. Sheep-farming was mainly carried out by manorial lords, whose rights included liberty of foldcourse, or by those to whom their sheep-walks had been let. Each flock was, in theory, confined to its own foldcourse, a well-defined area which normally included heaths and commons for spring and summer pasture, and arable land, of which the unsown portion provided communal grazing through autumn and winter. This arable land was half-year land.

Sheep appear early in the history of Runton. In 1086, d'Ecouis' land carried 60, while de Montfort's holding, to follow Blomefield, had 15. Both estates kept goats rather than sheep at Beeston.

Little evidence survives about conditions before the end of the 14th century. From then on people were frequently fined for causing damage in their neighbours' corn with their sheep and other animals; also for failure to maintain fallgates and fences adjoining the commons.

But it was already apparent that shepherds of the large manorial flocks were not very careful to keep to their own foldcourses. Twice in 1393 the shepherd of Felbrigg Hall, one John Wroughmowgth (surely the nickname of an abusive fellow) was reported to have violated the regulations of the Beeston manor in Runton. His flock had caused damage in the tenants' hay and corn, and had grazed illegally on the commons of that manor.

A century later – in 1491 and 1493 – some tenants were putting excessive numbers of sheep onto the commons. John Wynter, a manorial lessee, had 240 there, while two others jointly had 80.

But the 16th century was the time of the large flockmaster, the time when the foldcourse system was fully developed. In 1507 Thomas Wyndham of Felbrigg purchased an estate called Sextens, which included a foldcourse in Aylmerton, Felbrigg and Runton. At his death in 1522 he left his widow the income from

1,000 sheep for her lifetime, while reserving to his executors for seven years the sheep-walks in Runton and Aylmerton. In the same year, the operations of one of the largest sheep farmers in Norfolk impinged on the village: 'William Wilkyns, shepherd of Henry Fermour gent. in Crowmere, with his flock of sheep commoned over the East field of this manor in East Runton where they should not'.

Direct evidence of local flock management is only available from shepherds' accounts for the single year ending at Midsummer 1543. Sir Edmund Wyndham, who leased the manor of Beeston Regis but had not yet purchased Beeston Priory, kept under common control four flocks in this neighbourhood. Those at Aylmerton and Felbrigg each exceeded 900 wethers, while one ewe flock of about 600 was kept at Bromehall in Metton and another varying between 800 and 900 was at Runton. Other men's sheep were taken in as 'cullets' grazing with the wether flocks at twopence (1p) a head.

Later in the 16th century, Sir Francis Windham, Recorder of Norwich, inherited the Priory manor and leased that of Beeston Regis for £20 a year. An interesting sidelight on this rent is shown in a complaint he brought before the court of the Duchy of Lancaster in 1583. Peter Platten, Clement Wilkinson and Thomas Whynnet, none of them having freehold property worth 40 shillings (£2) a year, 'unlawfully kept Ferettes, nettes and other engyns to take Conyes with'. They had taken so many rabbits from his warren and had prevented the warreners from entering their lands that he was experiencing difficulty in raising his annual rent from the estate. Poaching had evidently gone down in the social scale: two centuries earlier the culprits, using dogs, had included local clergy and the famous Sir Thomas Erpingham.

A rental for Sir Francis Windham's properties in 1571 shows how tenants holding lands which that year lay within the foldcourse of the Beeston Regis manor were compensated for the grazing of the manorial flock. Of eight men concerned, six accepted an exchange of land for that year and the other two put sheep into the flock at a rate of about three per acre (0.4 hectare) affected. Some of these lands lay in other manors, e.g. Runton Hayes and Felbrigg's and Beeston Priory.

In February 1602/3, William Clapham, rector of Runton, was charged that he had denied to the Queen's lessees and their under-tenants freedom of sheep-walk for 800 sheep over his heathland; that he had sued them under Common Law and, more specifically, that within the last year he had deliberately enclosed 1½ acres (0.7 hecatre) of heathland to keep out the flock.

In his reply the rector acknowledged the royal right of foldcourse for 800 sheep. He stated that his enclosure was not within the manor of Beeston Regis, being part and parcel of Runton Stubbes. The court rolls of this manor show that in December 1600 he had paid the nominal sum of one penny for licence to enclose his 1½ acres. Clapham counter-attacked, saying that it was neither lawful

A shepherd with a cullet flock near Incleborough Hill, late in the nineteenth century.

nor reasonable for the 800 sheep 'to feed upp the Corne of the owners of severall [i.e. enclosed] lands within the said arrable fields everie yere' until Lady Day.
Praying that the case be dropped, he asked for his 'reasonable costs and charges
wrongfullie sustayned'.

Whether the case proceeded any further is not clear, for William Clapham died.
Certainly the matter must have been considered very important locally for a special court of Runton Stubbes, on 10th March 1602/3, dealt almost solely with the
practice in 'Justice Windams tyme'. Three pieces of land had been involved with
the passage of his flock. In two cases compensation had been paid, either in cash
or in permission to put a proportionate number of sheep into the flock. Regarding Clapham's 1½ acres it was stated 'that ther was no flocke to cum uppon this
piece but that he myght joine it if he woulde'. This verdict was of such importance that bound in with the minutes of the court is the sheet of paper bearing
the signatures or marks of the jurors.

Whether Clapham's argument could have prevailed is uncertain. Rentals and bailiffs' accounts of Runton Hayes and Felbrigg's manor in the 1630s and 1640s regularly
refer to one piece of land and two closes as lying within the Beeston foldcourse.

At the enquiry in 1976, conveyances of 1704 and 1751 were mentioned. Both referred to rights of sheep-walk and foldcourse on Abbey Farm, Beeston. It would seem that in the 17th century the right of foldcourse had become detached from the manorial lordship and attached to ownership of Abbey Farm. Henceforth there was no mention of the Beeston Regis manor in connection with the flock, but only Beeston Priory. However, in the valuation of the Priory made for Henry VIII in 1537 there is a nil return for pasture and no mention of sheep. Moreover, in the 1490s the prior was himself leasing from the Crown a foldage in West Runton.

The position in the 19th century was plainly stated in the sale particulars of the estate of the late Rev Paul Johnson in 1836: 'The half-year lands are subject to Sheep Walks and the Depasture of great and commonable cattle, from the 10th October to the 5th April and the Dole Lands [i.e. heaths] are also subject to a Sheep Walk for 400 sheep belonging to Beeston Abbey Farm, from the 5th April to the 10th October, in every year'.

A further amplification of the conditions was given in a paper read to the Norfolk and Norwich Archaeological Society in 1899. Grazing was restricted to daylight hours. Land sown with corn was exempted from the sheep, but that growing turnips was subject to a levy of two shillings (£0.10) an acre for the same privilege. The half-year lands of Runton, but not Beeston, were also subject to a right of shackage belonging to all occupiers of half-year lands, at the rate of 1½ sheep per acre of such holdings. These sheep were to be collected into one 'cullet' flock under a shepherd, but could not exercise their right on any land until the sheep-master's flock had passed over it. This was the theoretical right, but it was said that the stated proportions were not observed, while persons not occupying half-year lands had for very many years been in the habit of putting sheep in with the cullet flock.

In the same year, Erpingham Rural District Council convened a public meeting in Runton School 'to enquire into the customs and rights belonging to these Half-Year Lands'. Following this it was legal counsel's opinion that 'certainly the owners and occupiers of lands and houses in Runton, and probably the inhabitants of Runton, have a legal right to pasture all their sheep "levant and couchant" in Runton upon Half-Year lands and that the owners-in-fee of the Half-Year lands hold them subject to this right of pasturage'.

So armed, the District Council prosecuted a man who had begun building a house on the seaward side of Wyndham Park. On 26th June 1900 at the Law Courts, Judge Willis declared that 'there had existed in the inhabitants of Runton from time immemorial the rights claimed of pasturage on the Half-Year lands' and that this right could be legally enforced against the persons who owned the lands. He refused, however, to say whether the judgement would be binding in future cases. Following this case the District Council accepted compensation from owners who had infringed the Half-Year rights.

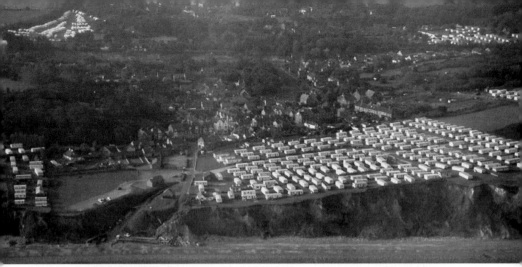

Any flight along the Norfolk coast reveals a startling number of caravans, as here at East Runton.

Not long after the judgement, Runton Parish Meeting actually voted in favour of abolishing the rights. In 1912, five of the larger property owners applied for a Provisional Enclosure Order, but this was refused.

During the agricultural recession of the inter-war years, summer camping sites became popular on land that had been let down to grass. With the increased mobility of people after World War 2, when caravan sites sprang up mainly, but not entirely, on the seaward side of the two villages. To avoid any suggestion of contravening the Half-Year rights the District Council issued licences which, in effect, respected the period of shackage. It was appreciated that the restrictions on uses inimical to grazing had retained the rural appearance of the parish.

However, in 1951, when some 18 acres (7.5 hectares) of the 100-year-old Fair Lady Plantation were clear-felled, there was no replanting because the land could not be enclosed with a fence against the rabbits on account of these rights. This was a rather ironic situation since the original plantation was reputedly protected by a fence made of barrel staves from the Spitalfields brewery, a Buxton family connexion. Indeed, one of the first acts of Sir Thomas Fowell Buxton, on purchasing the Johnson estate around the end of 1840, had been to plant trees on the dole lands and to fence them in. In a letter dated 25th February 1843, replying to a complaint by William Windham of Felbrigg, he acknowledged that this enclosure was 'by sufferance' of other owners who might have rights there. But he totally refused to pay even a nominal sum in compensation so as not to create a precedent.

When the enquiry came in 1976, the Commissioner's first act was to declare Judge Willis's decision *ultra vires*, and therefore not to be considered. Despite evidence regarding a cullet flock in 1913 under its shepherd, James 'Jimmy Dykey' Abbs, and an Abbey Farm flock which continued until the early 1920s with its own shepherd, 'Spuddy' Shepherd, it was clear to an impartial observer that the rights were as good as lost. So it proved.

One may wonder how it came to be believed that merely inhabiting Runton conferred the right to participate in the cullet flock. The following tentative suggestion is offered. In 1801 the total population of Runton was 312, being 60 households occupying 50 houses. It may well have been less in the 18th century. Most families would need a little land to feed a donkey or horse, and possibly a few other domestic animals. As occupants of half-year land they would be entitled to join the cullet flock, but if most families were in the same position then the distinction between the two capacities, occupiers of land and inhabitants of Runton, may have become blurred. The legal position was given in 1899, but custom is seldom written down, and we just do not know what transpired during the 17th and 18th centuries to transform what had been a resented privilege of manorial lordship into a cherished right of the inhabitants of Runton.

The church and some churchmen

The intimate connection between Runton and Beeston is exemplified in the case of the church, which stands almost on the parish boundary where it runs over the Mill Hill of the Beeston Regis manor.

In 1086 the church and its six acres were included in the measurement of William d'Ecouis' Beeston estate. A survey of the 1490s shows that the two parsonages lay side by side next to Runton church and that their glebe lands were similarly close together. In the case of the first 17 furlongs listed, mainly in the south-eastern part of East Runton, the tithes of numerous strips, usually belonging to the Crown manor, were payable to Beeston church and not to Runton.

The tithe maps of the two parishes show that in 1840 the glebe lands of each lay mainly in Runton; there and in Beeston they were generally contiguous. So one wonders about the origin of these arrangements – whether indeed it goes back beyond the Domesday Book, and whether there was originally one larger parish.

There are references in the late 15th century to a chapel in East Runton. Chapel Lane is noted in the 18th century, and Chapel Lane Close is the name given on the tithe map for a field where Brick Lane joins Thain's Lane. Faden's map of Norfolk, 1797, appears to call Top Common 'Chapel Green'. Nothing more is known at present.

The fabric of the church is described by the guide and by Pevsner and later writers. The financing of its construction would have been an enormous undertaking. If the tower is, as is supposed, of the 13th century and if the rest dates from the early 14th to the mid-15th century, then much of the work took place during a time of steady impoverishment – a time which included the Black Death. Governments do not readily grant tax rebates, but in 1449 Runton's assessment

The lower common, East Runton, at the end of the 19th century.

for the Lay Subsidy was reduced by 10 shillings – about 15%. It has been suggested that such reduced assessments were connected with manorial lords augmenting their own flocks of sheep at the expense of their tenants.

Whether the clergy raised funds or whether benefactors made large donations is not known. Blomefield states that there were in the church 'the arms of Felbrigg; Albiny Earl of Arundel, and Walcot'. Possibly these represented donors from among the manorial lords. Most of the wills surviving for Runton from the late 14th to the early 16th century made bequests for 'the reparation of the church', mainly in sums of say 20 pence (£0.08) or occasionally 13s 4d (£0.67).

Nicholas Marreys (or Mareys) was presented to the living in 1325 by the Prior of Beeston, who had the right of presentation alternately with the lord of Felbrigg's manor. In February 1332/3 the Patent Rolls record his acknowledgement of debts of £14 to William de Rodinton of Leicester and £20 to John Turveye. In each case payment in default was to be levied on his lands and chattels in Norfolk. One may wonder whether the borrowing was in any way connected with his church.

John Fenge, the rector who died in 1376, left 20 shillings (£2) for repairs and smaller sums for the churches of Weybourne, Sheringham, Beeston and Felbrigg.

His successor was Robert Stulle, who like several others bore the name of a local family. With three other inhabitants he became the lord of Runton Hayes manor in 1386. How this came about is not yet known, neither is the duration of his lordship. Possibly it had been granted to him temporarily as a form of almsgiving during the minority of an heir, just as the Beeston manor had been granted to the Prior of Beeston a century earlier. It may be that the profits and perquisites of the manor court were directed to rebuilding.

In 1388 Robert Stulle was reported to have harassed the tenants of the Beeston manor in the church courts. The physical condition of the parchment prevents us from discovering the actual charges, but the combination of both secular and religious authority in one man could easily have produced the equivalent of the 18th century 'squarson'. Certainly one incident in 1385 may carry some hint of undue influence on a dying man. Simon Aleyn, tenant of the Beeston manor, on his deathbed, made seven successive bequests of an acre or two, three of them to the parson and his feoffees. The property, amounting to about 6½ acres (2.7 hectares) and two messuages, was not retained as glebe but was sold within a few years.

At present little is known of the clergy of the 15th century. In 1401 Pope Boniface IV sanctioned the appropriation of Runton church and its endowments to Beeston Priory. The advowson (i.e. the right of presenting a parson to a benefice) of Runton and half that of Beeston were also granted to the Priory in 1412. Yet in 1416, in a Crown return of appropriated churches, Beeston Priory replied that they held no appropriations and that they had suffered much loss during the pestilence of 1349 and in a terrible inundation of 1400. So the canons of Beeston seem unlikely to have been able to contribute much towards any building work. Thomas Makke was the rector in 1428, but the monumental brass to one of that name now set into the altar-step of the south aisle is that of a substantial yeoman resident in Cromer at the time of his death in 1497, although evidently of Runton origin. In the latter year the parson, William Warner, seized and carried off 500 tiles from the land of one of his parishioners. He was fined 3 pence for setting a bad example, ordered to return the distrained goods before the next court and warned not to repeat the offence on pain of 20 shillings (£1).

Warner's successor, from 1499 to 1531, was John Everard, previously at Aylmerton and Felbrigg, retaining the latter cure until his death. His will shows that he had wide connections in Norwich and north Norfolk. It also states that his bequests, which are not specified, to Runton church and Cromer pier had already been carried out by his executor and successor, Robert Thorneham.

A very unusual entry in the rolls of the joint manor of Runton Hayes and Felbrigg's for 1540 concerns Thorneham and Roger Skottowe, whose Beeston parsonage house adjoined that of Runton. Both were presented for behaving unlawfully and suspiciously with harlots in their houses. Fined two shillings each, they were ordered to mend their ways and warned not to repeat the offence on pain of 20 shillings. Next year Skottowe was fined 20 shillings for repetition of his conduct and placed under a further penalty of 30 shillings. Other court rolls and the wills of the two men suggest that the charges were not without foundation.

It would seem that the church may not always have been dedicated to the Holy

A general view of West Runton in the first decade of the 20th century.

Trinity. Most testators, even before the Reformation, refer only to the parish church of Runton as their chosen place of burial. However, of 40 wills surviving from the period between 1469 and 1561, 14 specifically refer to the church of Our Lady or the Blessed Virgin Mary of Runton. Possibly a change of dedication was made following the reign of Mary I.

Whether the church had suffered much damage during the so-called Great Pillage is not known, but it was stated to be in a ruinous condition in December 1554, the year of Mary's marriage to Philip of Spain. At least that was the reason advanced when permission was given for the union of the benefice to Aylmerton for the incumbency of Edmund Windham. However, this may merely have been a ploy to profit one whose precise relationship to Sir Edmund Windham (or Wyndham) is a matter of conjecture. In 1569 both the rectory and the chancel were reported to be in great ruin, and the rector non-resident. How long Windham remained is not clear, for he was a papist.

Runton seems to have been well involved in one of the religious disputes of the late 16th century, a controversy about the wearing of special vestments. At Bishop Scambler's visitation in 1593, eleven charges were raised by one of the churchwardens, Thomas Whynnet, against the rector, William Clapham. He did not read Common Prayer; nor service on Wednesdays and Fridays; he did not wear the surplice as appointed by the book of Common Prayer; he did not catechise, nor bid fasting days; he was not resident upon his parsonage; he was not peaceable; he did not keep the register; he went to harrow, yet the parsonage barn was in ruins; and finally he refused to christen Whynnet's child on the Sabbath.

The rector rebutted these charges. He could not wear a surplice as there was only an old one, very torn. As to the non-christening of the child, Whynnet had refused to let him do so, saying that no knave should baptize his child. The barn had burned down before his institution; and he bestowed a large part of the income of his benefice on repairs to the chancel and the parsonage houses. At Bishop Redman's visitation in 1597 there is no separate entry for Runton, so presumably Clapham conformed. However, his will made in 1603 shows that he remained an extreme Protestant, indeed a Calvinist. It is a very long and detailed document in which Clapham made many charitable bequests, both locally and in his native Yorkshire. Among other items it established an almshouse and supporting charity in Runton. One small bequest which must be viewed in the light of the religious atmosphere of the times was 'to the Townsmen and Wyves of Runton 20 shillings to make them merry withall in lent next after my death'. To one of Clapham's persuasion anything, such as ritualised grief, that smacked of Rome would have been anathema.

It was after all only 15 years since the Spanish Armada had threatened the kingdom. Clergy, just as laymen, had to show a certain amount of armour at musters of the Militia. While it is probable that Clapham's store may have belonged to his wife's first husband the list is quite impressive. The inventory of his goods and chattels, valued at £624 5s 4d, included: in the study, 'two calivers [light muskets], two musketts, one fully furnyshed, one fowling peece, a Curate [cuirass or body armour] furnyshed, one staffe, one blacke bill, two brush hooks, one old pistoll, two longe bowes, one stone bowe, two scottishe Daggers, two swords, two daggers, one gauntlet and one half pyke', and in the low combe [dormer] chamber, 'a sheiffe of arrowes'. Similarly, Clapham's successor, William Flemynge, later rector of Beeston as well, left in his effects 'one Corslett [body armour] furnyshed'.

In 1622 John Furmary was instituted rector of both Beeston and Runton. A Royalist, he was removed from his cure during the Civil War, and when he made his will in September 1643 was a prisoner in Buckenham Castle. Presumably he was not held there very long because the Committee for Plundered Ministers in February 1646/7 deferred hearing his case until May on account of his age and inability to travel to London in winter. He had, however, already been termed the late rector. It seems likely that Furmary was reinstated at the Restoration of 1660, since his will was not proved until 15th June 1661. A new rector, Roger Flint, was presented by John Windham, the patron, at the end of June 1661 and instituted a month later. According to Blomefield, Flint, another Royalist, had been ejected from three benefices during the Commonwealth period.

In 1648, during Furmary's enforced absence, Edward Worsley, brother of one of Cromwell's major generals, became rector of both Runton and Beeston and, after the Restoration, was appointed to the living at Letheringsett. Two of his letters to his father have been published and shed some light on the harshness of conditions. In April 1649 he wrote of the very high price of corn, with wheat and

Runton church as depicted by Ladbrooke in the early 1820s

rye at twice the normal rate. In February 1650/1, he complained of government charges and taxes being much greater than previously, with money scarce and the return on corn 'indifferent'. His last two months' tax assessment had been more than £3, while the corn merchant with whom he dealt had failed and decamped, owing the rector over £5.

Following all the ferment of the 16th and 17th centuries, the church at Runton seems to have slumbered and slowly decayed. In the 19th century, much-needed repairs were carried out, but the result was the loss of some of the remaining medieval character – including the lower half of the screen. William Clapham had left £10 for the erection, on the north side of the chancel door, of a tomb three feet high to house his leaden coffin. Such a tomb, with the brass missing, apparently existed on the north side of the chancel in the early 19th century but is now no more.

As may be seen from Ladbrooke's lithograph, executed before 1825, there were formerly four clerestory windows on the south side of the nave. The scars resulting from the removal of two buttresses supporting the wall of the south aisle can still be seen. Whether a second small perpendicular window there was uncovered or inserted is unclear. Perhaps the artist's recording is at fault. The opening up of the large perpendicular windows in the chancel to their full height must have vastly improved the internal lighting. The north porch, in ruins in 1840, was converted into a vestry.

The rising tide of nonconformity in the 19th century brought about the building of a Primitive Methodist chapel at East Runton in 1845. This was enlarged in

1897 by the construction of the present chapel, which retained half of the original as a schoolroom. The Methodist chapel at West Runton, replacing a wooden building, was erected in 1951 as a memorial to Willie Long, fisherman-evangelist, a lay preacher widely known and respected in fishing ports.

In July 1958 Runton school was closed. The owners, successors to the Buxtons, agreed to sell the buildings to the Parochial Church Council for conversion to a church, which would replace a wooden ex-army hut situated at the other end of Lower Common. On 6th August 1959, St Andrew's Church was dedicated. But after only a few years the escalating costs of maintaining a century-old building became too great and the major part was auctioned off, leaving only the former infant's school-room and lobby as the church. While the major part of the building became a private house, since 1988 it has housed St Andrew's School where a number of children with communication difficulties are taught. On the 7th August 1957 a rather utilitarian village hall built on the former school gardens, where boys had learned the rudiments of growing vegetables, was opened by E. G. Gooch, the local MP. It has since been enlarged.

The community: people and places

Most figures for population before the first census in 1801, whose accuracy has sometimes been doubted, are of necessity 'guesstimates', involving the application of some theoretical multiplier to lists made for some other purpose, usually taxation.

If one accepts Blomefield's view of the holdings in 1086, there were 44 men, possibly heads of households. Under Roger Bigot were 2 freemen, 5 villeins and 2 bordars; under William d'Ecouis 10 bordars and 5 socmen; and under Hugh de Montfort 12 bordars and 8 socmen. However, if the last holding is taken to have been in Roughton, then the total is only 24.

Walter Rye published two Subsidy Rolls for the early years of the reign of Edward III. In 1327, 37 people, mainly men, paid 57 shillings. This list includes William Haye, possibly the last manorial lord actually to reside in the vill. In 1332, 38 persons paid 60 shillings and 2 pence. From 1334 the figure was fixed at an arbitrary sum of 66 shillings and 2 pence, until 1449 when a reduction of 10 shillings was made on account of impoverishment.

Some clue as to the severity of the Black Death in Runton may be gained from the court rolls of Runton Hayes manor. On 17th February 1348/9 a court was held for Robert de Reppes. The next one was held nine months later, on 19th November 1349, on behalf of his widow, Dame Alice. It dealt with land transfers resulting from the recent deaths of 21 tenants, male and female, many of whose surnames appear on the earlier Subsidy Rolls. As Runton Hayes was one of the smaller manors, with around 10% of the land, the death toll for the whole vill must have been considerably greater, although it is recognised that some people may have held land from more than one manor as they did at the end of the 15th century.

In the early part of the reign of Richard II Runton was affected, like most of Norfolk, by the unrest precipitated by fresh Poll Tax demands and which culminated in the so-called Peasants' Revolt of 1381. One of the objects of this Rising of the Commons, as it was then termed, was the destruction of manorial archives which recorded, among other things, a person's status, bond or free, and obligations in rent and services. Few local documents survive from earlier periods, but the court rolls of Runton Hayes, in a somewhat broken series from 1281, record nothing special during 1381 or the next few years. The rolls for Beeston-iuxta-Mare (later Regis) do not commence until 1384, which may imply destruction of the records. However, those of Runton Felbrigg's begin in October 1381 with a heading stating that this was the first court held since the burning of the manorial archives 'by the Commons of the Country'. A certain amount of passive disobedience is noted, such as refusal to perform labour services. One man, however, had made his own demonstration of disaffection. Robert Bully was a villein tenant of the Beeston manor, in whose court he came to hold minor office, but he also held land of Runton Felbrigg's. He had driven his horses, cows and sheep to and fro over demesne land of the latter at Holgate, 'so reducing to nothing the corn growing there' that barley estimated at 1 quarter 4 bushels and worth 3s 6d was destroyed. He was also fined a similar amount for making an unlawful track there.

The way in which the organisation of the township worked is not yet understood. Each of the five main manors undoubtedly had its own court concerned with tenurial matters and its leet dealing with minor offences. In particular, each of the three for which evidence of late medieval practice is available appointed its own ale-tasters, and fined, or in effect licensed, its own brewers of ale and retailers of bread. The same ale-tasters and brewers do not appear in those capacities in the rolls of more than one manor, so that some territorial division must be assumed, but cannot be demonstrated. Similarly, the Beeston manor appointed a reeve annually in turn from East Runton, West Runton and Beeston. But whether he was just a manorial official or had some oversight over the three villages is not known, since no mention of a man acting in the capacity of reeve has yet been found. As far as can be seen the basic organisation of a manor at grassroots was the responsibility of the messor, or hayward. A bond tenant, this man was answerable to the court for the performance of his duties but was not elected by it, and so must be presumed to have been a direct appointee of the lord or his steward.

At present, conditions during the 15th century remain unclear, but a survey of Runton relating to the 1490s does shed some light on the subject. From this field-book, it appears that there were then about 81 dwellings, including the adjoining parsonages of Runton and Beeston, together with two or three houses in ruins. Rentals for two of the manors at the end of the 16th century showed a net increase of 8 dwellings on their lands, while 16 others were in ruins or had been absorbed into larger houses. This would suggest a possibility of around 100 houses at that time. However, in 1603 the ecclesiastical Return of Communicants, presumably all persons over 16, numbered only 153.

Some 70 years later two other returns are no easier to correlate. In 1676, the Compton religious census gives 80 as the number of communicants, there being no nonconformists or papists. The Hearth Tax returns for this period, which list the number of fireplaces per house, are not well preserved. Using a conflation of several figures, J. H. C. Patten showed that in 1674 there were 17 taxpayers and between 43 and 51 poor persons, say 60 to 68 households.

The earliest, and badly kept, parish register for Runton commences in 1743. From that time until the first census of 1801, baptisms exceeded burials by about 250. The actual increase in population would, of course, have been much less than this, for allowance has to be made for probable emigration, whether within Britain or abroad, for loss at sea of fishermen and other mariners, and also for the likely absence of men in the long Napoleonic war. In view of this increase, the 1801 figure of 312 persons, comprising 60 households living in 50 houses, one being vacant, seems to imply that the population had dwindled to a very small size by the middle of the 18th century.

In 1765, a return of those eligible for service in the militia was required. All men between 18 and 45 years of age were to be listed, except certain categories of office-holder, seafarers and such poor men as had three legitimate children. In the event, 20 names were given, two being over age and five coming within the various exceptions, so that only 13 able-bodied men were left as eligible.

To return to the 16th century, the scope of the tax known as the Lay Subsidy was widened in the 1520s. In that for 1524/5, which was based on a return made ostensibly for military purposes, 45 persons, including two women, were assessed at a total of £3 3s 6d. Of this number, nine were rated on their land, 18 on their movable goods, and 18 were wage earners. Fifteen of the last group were paid at the lowest rate of 4d, which is held to indicate a poor man. The only trade mentioned is that of shipwright, represented by Peter and John Platting. The number of taxpayers declined in subsequent years until only five men had to raise £3 in 1551/2.

During the first quarter of the 17th century there were official reports of the presence of Dunkirkers off the coast of East Anglia harassing the local shipping with acts of piracy and privateering. An interesting document in the Norfolk Record Office is entitled 'This booke doth shewe what some every severall Corporacion or parishe or towne within the county of Norffolke was rated unto the furnishinge of the first Shippe of war 1635'. This refers to the hated tax, Ship

Money. Interestingly, Runton was assessed at £7 3s 6d., Beeston at £3 19s 6d, Sheringham at £7 19s 0d, but Cromer at only £4 4s 8d. The really wealthy places in the Hundred of North Erpingham were Northrepps and Southrepps, each rated at over £18. During the herring season that year, there were said to be 1,000 Dutch sail off the Norfolk coast.

Harvests were poor in Norfolk during the 1620s, while in 1640 the Sheriff of Norfolk, Sir Thomas Windham, reported 'a general damp of industry'. The poverty of the time is illustrated by a rental of Runton Stubbes manor for 1645. In two cases, copyhold land, which should have descended by inheritance, was 'now letten to fearme [i.e. leased] by reason there would not any come to take them upp because the fine [i.e. entry premium] and charges come to soe much'.

Bailiffs' accounts of the Runton Hayes and Felbrigg's manor show that rents of lands leased out were sharply increased in 1635. For example, Richard Dawson's rent for 1½ acres was two shillings in 1634, but next year a new agreement raised it to 7s 6d, plus 1 hen and 1 day's labour. Similarly, Christopher Rooke's payment of 5s 0d for 2½ acres was increased to 12 shillings, also plus 1 hen and 1 day's labour.

References to national events seldom occur in manorial records, but the same bailiffs' accounts show that some of these lessees had been paying 'parliament charges' on their land. In 1648, Christopher Rooke was allowed a rebate of 13½d in this respect; while at the end of the interregnum, the Widow Feazer

Vessels on the shore at East Runton. Cromer church and jetty can be seen in the background.

was allowed 3s 6d and Thomas Swift 1s 6d for payments they had made up to Michaelmas 1660.

Reminders of external dangers, from the Dutch, are to be found in the Order Books of the Norfolk Quarter Sessions from 1650 onwards. In January 1652 it was ordered that all beacons in the county were to be maintained and watched, as indeed they had been in the 1620s. For the repair and watching of those at Trimingham and Runton, £10 was to be raised in the Hundreds of Mitford and North and South Erpingham. Next year they were each watched at night by one man paid sixpence a night, the county having to raise £200 in respect of 12 beacons.

By 1665, no account had been rendered regarding the disbursement of this sum. A further £200 had to be raised for repairs, and in 1666 another £150 for watching the beacons. The account for these last sums, date 30th July 1668, shows that £4 14s 0d was spent by Sir Thomas Rant on repairing, and £18 12s 6d by a Mr Gay on watching Runton beacon.

Where was this beacon? It seems to have been liable to fall quickly into disuse and disrepair. Human memory being what it is, the comments of M. J. Armstrong in his *History and Antiquities of the County of Norfolk*, 1781, should come as no surprise. Referring to a small ruined building about a half a mile north of Aylmerton church, called the Iron Beacon from the material of its construction, he wrote 'At this momentous crisis, when an invasion of our country is threatened by the House of Bourbon, this building, if properly supplied, would be an excellent alarm-beacon, if occasion required'.

There is little doubt that this is what is now called the Roman Camp, in the banks of which iron slag is found as a component. The modern name is believed to have been coined around the turn of the 19th century by a horse-cab driver as a suitably romantic destination for an afternoon's drive. This may have been inspired by the booklet, *Guide to Cromer and its Neighbourhood*, 3rd edition, by a Visitor, where reference is made to a 'spot . . . on top of the heath, which by some, is stated to have been a Roman encampment, but it is much more probable the site of an ancient beacon'.

The site is near what was, at 329 feet, regarded the highest point in Norfolk, until metrication of the Ordnance Survey maps demoted it to second place, below Pigg's Grave near Melton Constable. Such a prominent position may well have been used for the same purpose by the Romans, but real proof of that is lacking.

Maps from the turn of the 18th century onwards show it for what it was. Thus Faden, 1797, terms it 'Old Beacon' or 'Watch Tower'. Bryant, 1826, marks it as 'Telegraph Station'. The first one-inch Ordnance Survey map, 1838, calls it 'Signal Station' and shows it standing on 'Black Beacon Hills'. The unpublished two-inch drawing prepared for the Ordnance Survey in 1816 labels it 'Runton Signal House', others being sited at Trimingham and on Kelling Heath. Runton tithe map, 1840, locates it on 'Telegraph Dole' while the first six-inch Ordnance

Survey map, prepared in 1885, marks it simply as 'Beacon Hill'.

It seems likely then, that the banks visible today are the remains of a signal station dating from the Napoleonic war, part of a chain running along the south and east coasts from Devon up to Edinburgh. Those from Norfolk downwards were ordered to be 'broken up' in November 1814, but those in the south and south-east were reactivated the next year. Both the tithe map and the first one-inch Ordnance Survey map show a 'Gun House', situated in the open fields north of the coast road near Wet Acre. Possibly this also may have been a relic of the French Wars, for its position could command Woman Hithe and Goss's Gap, just as the battery on the Marram Hills at Cromer no doubt commanded East Runton Gap and the approach to Cromer itself.

The 19th century and later

That event of the 19th century which had the most lasting impact on Runton was undoubtedly the purchase of the estate of the late Rev. Paul Johnson by Sir Thomas Fowell Buxton, Bart. of Bellfield, Dorset, and Runton, Norfolk. Buxton, who had succeeded William Wilberforce as leader of the campaign for the Abolition of Slavery, died only a few years after this acquisition, but he had begun a process of development which was continued by his descendants. Familiar with the parish through long enjoyment of shooting rights here and in the neighbourhood, he had previously owned only a few acres. Now in late 1840 or early 1841, by the purchase of some 475 acres he instantly became the major landowner and, with his successors, continued to acquire more land. During his last few years, Sir Fowell, as he was usually called, continued, when in Norfolk, to reside at Northrepps Hall, which he had rented since 1828, but set up model farms at Trimingham and Runton. Here he established a sporting estate, his gamekeeper being the Irishman Larry Banville. He made coverts and plantations, giving at least two of them, Fernando (Po) and Niger, names connected with his work for the Abolition of Slavery.

As noted elsewhere, Buxton was unapologetic about fencing-in the dole-lands. The attitude of the commoners towards this is not known. It may be that any objection to possible loss of ancient rights was outweighed by sheer necessity. The new woods provided much-needed work in that bitter decade known as the Hungry Forties.

It may now be appropriate to introduce a little oral tradition about conditions in the 19th century. There has long been a rather unlikely tale handed down in the writer's family. James Leak (or Leake or Lake) was a blacksmith and a bare-knuckle fighter of local repute. The tithe survey shows that he lived in one of six houses on the cliff at East Runton in 1840, while White's *Directory* of 1845 states that his forge was at West Runton. The story goes that he had a toe which was either gangrenous or in danger of becoming so. In desperation he put his foot on the anvil, took a chisel and cut off the toe, cauterizing the stump with a red-hot iron. Corroboration of this improbable story has been provided by *The Banville Diaries*, 1986, which quoted a report in the *Norwich Mercury* of 24th February 1827. Apparently the blacksmith, being unable to afford a surgeon's fees, had coolly made a special implement with which to perform the operation himself. It seems that everything went well, for he continued his prize fighting and lived to be 82.

Other, less dramatic, strands of family tradition relate to Oxwell Cross. At one time, drinking water was brought by cart from the spring there and sold in East Runton at a farthing a pailful. This spring served as a place of refreshment for workers in the harvest-fields nearby and also for bearers carrying the dead for burial in the parish churchyard. Apparently it was the men's custom to stop at Oxwell Cross and place the coffin under a rough shelter that stood on the little common on the south side of the road, while they slaked their thirst from the pure, but very cold, water of the spring on the other side. This may, indeed, be an unconscious echo of pre-Reformation custom, since a survey of the 1490s locates the actual cross in a small plot of land on the south side of the place to which it had given its name.

While the tithe apportionment of 1840 makes no reference to a school, both the census of 1841 and White's *Directory* of 1845 mention a schoolmistress, though not the same person. Some sort of dame school may have been involved. The cottage next to the Old Hall is said to have been used for that purpose at one time.

Whether the Buxtons were involved in education from the beginning of their period in Runton is unclear, but the second baronet, Sir Edward North Buxton, in 1852 built a school-room on land adjoining Lower Common, East Runton. In the year of his death, 1858, a larger Gothic-style building was erected at right angles to the first room. Education was conducted on the principles of the National Schools. A further extension on the north side of the second room was built in 1911.

For more than 80 years the Buxton family, having considerably enlarged its original estate, was the dominating influence in Runton. Besides the school, a men's reading room, to which a billiard room was later added, was provided in East Runton, as well as a fishermen's shelter near the Gangway. Sir E. N. Buxton was closely concerned in the restoration of the church in the 1850s. So firmly indeed was the family associated with the parish that a piece of W. H. Goss's crested china, labelled 'The Manor of Runton', actually bears the Buxton arms.

The house which later became a Buxton residence in Runton is called 'Wright's Farm' in the 1841 census and 'Peartree Farm' in directories of 1868 and 1869, the name 'Runton Old Hall' not appearing until 1875. In 1910/11, the building was extensively remodelled and enlarged for Bertram Hawker, who had married into the family. The architect was Bailie Scott, while Gertrude Jekyll laid out the gardens. To facilitate the alterations, a road diversion was necessary. In 1909, Brick Kiln Lane, which varied in width from 12 to 18 feet and ran close to the western side of the house, was stopped up for a length of 160 yards. It was replaced by the present road, 18 feet wide including a path, running diagonally for 235 yards to a point near the Brick Works. This was properly called 'New Road', but that name has been forgotten, the whole now being just 'Brick Lane'.

In the application for the road diversion, no mention was made of advantages accruing to the owners of the Old Hall, but only of the benefits to the inhabitants of the village, most of whom were said to live to the north and north-east of the site. Traffic from Felbrigg would be saved 4 yards, while that from the northern part of East Runton would have 72 yards less to travel! The year 1909 also saw the completion of the sewerage system in East Runton, which may have been not unrelated to the other work.

However, the people of Runton must by now have become used to gigantic alterations to their familiar surroundings. They had seen gangs of 'navigators' dig the cuttings and make the embankments of the railway line from Holt to Cromer, which was inaugurated on 16th June 1887. West Runton station was opened in September of that year. Then, on 23rd July 1906, the Runton West–Newstead Lane junction, with an even higher embankment and a five-span bridge, was put to work, so completing the triangle that carves up East Runton. This last link was closed on 21st April 1963, leaving the viaduct as a monument in a conservation area.

The coming of the railway caused changes in the parish, stimulating building as

Victoria Terrace in East Runton

East Runton: the buildings remain today, though the traffic and fashions have cha...

its promoters no doubt intended. Fifty years after the first census, the number of inhabitants had risen from 312 to 485, and the houses from 51 to 112, a dozen of these since 1841. For the next thirty years the population rose and fell, being 506 in 1881, when there were 118 dwellings. In 1891, four years after the coming of the railway, there were 601 people and 141 houses, with 8 more under construction. Corresponding figures for 1901 were 840 people and 199 houses, of which 13 were vacant, while 5 more were being built.

The progress of these building surges can be seen today. At West Runton several houses bear the date 1847, while others were built in 1891, notably the imposing Runton House, which replaced what had formerly been Beeston Rectory. The Links Hotel has a plaque dated 1899; its associated Golf Club celebrated its centenary in 2003. At East Runton, with no station of its own, the tendency seems to have been to absorb the overflow of Cromer's holiday trade. From this period there are several terraces of houses built either expressly for boarding visitors or readily adaptable for the purpose. Further expansion took place at West Runton in the 1920s, when shops were built on the south side of the Street.

It is rather surprising to find that the Village Inn was not opened until 9th September 1927, for even in medieval times West Runton had at least two ale houses. At East Runton, the Fishing Boat has a much longer history. As the 'Boat

Boulevard Road, West Runton

Public House', it appears on the tithe map of 1840, and it was there that the manorial court of Runton Stubbes met in 1816. In 1734 this court was held at the 'Three Horse Shoes', which may have been an earlier name. The White Horse seems to date from 1851, when the court book of Beeston Priory manor records that Ambrose Mayes sold to William Primrose, brewer, of Trunch, '21 perches of land on which a messuage or dwelling house and other buildings have lately been erected and built'. In September that year, Primrose was admitted, as tenant of the manor, to 'a messuage or Public House called the White Horse and other edifices . . . on the same piece'.

Charity

It is generally assumed that before the Reformation the relief of the poor and needy was performed by religious establishments such as monasteries. How far this is true of Beeston Priory is not known, but other religious houses which held manors were not particularly benevolent towards their tenants. However, in the last twenty years before the Dissolution, one finds two of the priors and a senior canon acting as witnesses, executors or supervisors of the wills of local testators.

Of about 30 pre-Reformation wills of people having ties with Runton, practically all made bequests towards the maintenance of the church. Twenty-four left small sums to one or more of the three gilds there – those of Our Lady, St Anne and St John the Baptist; and 11 to the Plough Light. A few left a little money to be distributed either immediately on their death, or spread over two or three years, for distribution among the poorest people.

The gilds were, of course, religious associations of people for mutual help and benefit, concerned in some measure to provide proper burial for fellow members. They are sometimes seen as distant precursors of Friendly Societies. The situation seems less clear regarding the Plough Light. Blomefield states that this light was 'maintained by old, and young persons who were husbandmen, before some image, and on Plough Monday [i.e. the Monday following 6th January] had a feast, went about with a plough, and some dancers to support it'. The Plough Light may, indeed, be remembered in the name of the Ploughlet Charity, which was usually distributed early in the New Year, but now during December. After the suppression of the gilds in 1547, few wills of the later 16th century make any provision for charity other than small donations to the 'poor men's box of East Runton' or a 'penny dole' to each pauper attending the testator's funeral.

In 1603, the Rector of Runton for 20 years, William Clapham, died and by his will, a fascinating document making numerous charitable bequests both in Norfolk and his native Yorkshire, founded a charity to maintain an almshouse. To his executors he left 'my howse in east Runton with the landes thereto belonging which I purchased of William Dingle to thend & purpose that the same shall remaine & be for ever to the use of the Towne of Runton aforesaid for the placeing inhabiting & relieving of two poor folkes be they single or coopled'. The trustees were to be the owners of his capital messuage and the Constables of Runton, who were to use the profit from the rents of the land for the relief and maintenance of those placed in the house. This land amounted in all to just over nine acres.

In 1713, Robert Feazer of West Runton, by his will, left 2½ acres on the cliff at East Runton in trust to his son and son-in-law, subject to the following condition. On 1st January every year they should distribute the clear yearly rent amongst the 'poor widows and old maids of East and West Runton not taking alms of the said parish'. This trust was taken up in December 1717.

Edmund Hooke, sometime Mayor of King's Lynn, by his will of June 1715, directed his executor to lay out £100 on the purchase of land, the clear rent of which should be used to provide fuel for the poor of Beeston Regis and Upper Runton, two thirds to the former and one third to the latter. Land was bought in Hindolveston for this purpose in about 1733.

When particulars of charities were returned to the House of Commons under Gilbert's Act in 1786, memory had become hazy. While Hooke was mentioned, Clapham's name had been forgotten and that of Robert Feazer had been changed to Miss Feazer, spinster. Reference was also made to land given by Thomas Smith, this land producing nearly two-thirds of the total income of £15 3s 9d.

It is a commonplace that land or money left to charity was very often misappropriated or silently absorbed into the holdings of the trustees. Runton was no exception. In 1811, Zachary Clark published a book on Norfolk charities, based on the returns of 1786 and on his own research in the diocesan archives. He was critical of the low return from the land held by the charities, and also of the fact that none of the donations or benefactions was recorded in the glebe terriers. Whether or not as a result of this publication, the court of Beeston Regis manor,

'Runton near Cromer', painted by James Stark in 1834. It is difficult to give a precise location.

on 6th November 1811, made a first proclamation (normally three were made at successive sessions) that the trustees for the Poor of the Town of Runton, who had taken up a tenement of half an acre in West Runton in 1730, had been dead for some time. Nothing further was heard of this piece of land.

In November 1783, James Everett, mariner, and his wife, Elizabeth, gave a cottage with its appurtenances for use by the Churchwardens and Overseers of the Poor of East Runton as a dwelling for the poor of the parish. This cottage, or its replacement, still stands on Top Common. Among the trustees were Paul Johnson, gentleman, and his son, Paul Johnson, clerk.

The court book shows that, in November 1807, Rev. Paul Johnson and two other remaining trustees surrendered this property to the use of the said Rev. Paul Johnson, as the phrase goes. It was among the properties advertised for sale in 1836 after his death. Admittedly, it is not known what price, fair or not, was paid, but it was the sort of irregularity which the later Enquiry would have viewed unfavourably.

From the late 17th to the early 19th century, the trustees, churchwardens and overseers of the poor were drawn mainly from a small grouping of locally influential families (Smith, Goss, Woodrow, Johnson, Beales, Pank, Breese). They appear not always to have been as correct and assiduous in their unpaid duties as might have been desired.

Rev. Paul Johnson senior, rector of Beeston Regis, owned probably the largest estate in Runton and lived in what is now Incleborough House. The oddly shaped extension of the grounds of this house into Lower Common in is fact an encroachment for which he was fined 2*s* 6*d* at a court of the Beeston Regis manor on 16th November 1808. He was ordered to restore the land to its former state by 6th April 1809 on pain of forfeiting 40 shillings. No further reference to this occurs in the record. Local tradition, however, has it that land at Sparrow's Park was given in exchange, but documentary evidence has so far proved elusive.

At the court of Beeston Priory manor, held on 6th December 1811, it was reported as in the case of the other Beeston manor, that the former trustees for the inhabitants of Runton and those for the poor widows and old maids of Runton, admitted in 1724 and 1717 respectively, had died some time since. New men, from the usual 'principal inhabitants', were appointed.

Meanwhile, at Holt and Letheringsett, the Inclosure Commissioners in 1810 set out just under 21 acres to the trustees for the Poor of Runton. The 1786 return had referred to one donation by Thomas Smith, and it seems likely that it was represented by this land, which at a later date contained a wood known as "Runton's Poor". Unfortunately, the Smith family had a succession of five or six heirs named Thomas from 1612 to 1728 and it has not been possible so far to find and check all their wills to discover which, if any, of them was the donor.

Thus, when the Commissioners for Inquiring Concerning Charities reported on Runton and Beeston Regis in 1834, two of the three Runton charities were described as 'donor unknown'. The Feazer bequest was accurately recorded. Their report was not wholly favourable. They noted that the land at Holt and Letheringsett was heath and was capable of improvement if a suitably covenanted lease were arranged. From Hooke's charity in Beeston, which for 28 years had been under the sole management of one man, a fixed amount of £1 13s was received, whereas one third of the clear income should then have been £4 13s 4d. They also noted that two tenants of the Poor Lands were trustees of the charity, and they referred to the need to 'avoid suspicion' by letting to tender, despite the manner in which some lands lay among other men's holdings. Furthermore, they described as 'a useless and improper application of the money' the practice of spending about 12s 6d on beer both for those receiving and those distributing the charity.

Matters seem to have drifted along much as before until 1883, when the old charities, known collectively as the Ploughlet Charity, were regulated by a scheme of the Charity Commissioners. At that time only two trustees remained, Rev. Paul Johnson junior, who stated that he had never acted in the administration, and his brother, Herbert J. Johnson, solicitor at Cromer. The latter was the 'Lawyer Johnson' of a piece of doggerel current at the end of the century:

> *'Now here's a job', said Bully Bob.*
> *'He burnt his books', said old Mrs Brooks.*
> *'A load of nonsense', said Lawyer Johnsons.*

It is not known whether there were any more couplets or what gave rise to them. 'Bully Bob' would be fisherman and sometime lifeboat coxswain 'Bully Bob' Allen, and Mrs Brooks was landlady of the Albion public house in Cromer.

Of Johnson himself, suffice it to say that comments about him in *The Banville Diaries* come as no surprise.

With the establishment of the regulated Ploughlet Charity, the use of a double cottage at East Runton as an almshouse was abandoned, if this had not already been done. All the properties thus became an income-producing endowment, and so continue.

Place names

The number of places, lanes, greens, hills and other topographical features that can be traced by name back to the Middle Ages is very small indeed. The tithe map of 1840, the earliest large-scale map of the parish, is of little help because most of its names seem to be of relatively recent origin, bearing little relation to contemporaneous records in manor court books, which generally perpetuate the names of long-dead occupiers and obsolete descriptions. It has proved almost impossible to correlate with the tithe map a detailed survey of the furlongs and strips of land which made up the field system of Runton in the late 15th century. This is not really surprising in view of an endorsement made in 1777 on the Beeston glebe terrier (list of lands with which the church was endowed). This was to the effect that the ancient descriptions had been repeated because the signatories did not know the exact boundaries, many Mier Baulks having been from time to time ploughed up and destroyed'.

Holgate (1382), Oxwell Crosse, Pothill and Woman Hythe Gappe (all late 15th century) are among the names to come through unchanged, although Woman Hithe furlong adjoined Pot Hill and so may properly relate to Goss's Gap before the sea had claimed so much land. Still recognizable from the 1490s are: Wynkyllborrow, or Wynkelburgh, for Incleborough Hill; Colgryme (and Colgrim, 1603), for Congham Hill; Curres Well, for Calves Well; while le Hyrne is noted in 1538. Seagate (1382) in various forms, is Beach Road, formerly Cliff Lane, in East Runton. Medowe Lane in West Runton is now Water Lane. Churchegate Streete (1490s) in West Runton is self-evident.

The various greens and commons seem to have changed names fairly frequently. The Common of West Runton was usually referred to as such, although it may perhaps have been called Westgate Grene (1501) or Kirkegate Grene. At East Runton, South Grene and Kergate Grene are noted in the late 14th century and Bennett's Green in the 16th, but these have not yet been placed. Certainly Top Common was referred to as East Runton Grene in 1521, but occurs in 1552 as Reyman's Grene alias Netillgrene alias Kartegate Grene, while Faden's map of 1797 appears to call it Chapel Green. The 1841 census terms it Wright's Common. Lower Common may have been Corgate (or perhaps Kergate) Green.

It is possible that the main road, or King's Highway, between East and West Runton ran via Thain's Lane (a recent name) to Incleborough Hill and thence towards the church. What is now the coast road was in the late 15th century merely a common way from each village to Oxwell Cross.

Even on the tithe map, the Holt road leaving Cromer and forming part of Runton's south-east boundary was still known as Cuckoo Lane. Spelt 'Cuckow' in the 18th century, this name probably derives from a hill, Guckehowgh (1490s), where several closes called Guckhow in the late 16th century had also become 'Cuckow' in the mid-18th. The name may perhaps be recalled in the woodland, Swacking Cuckoo, which lies on the Cromer–Felbrigg boundary just south of the Holt road.

As a name, Wood Hill may not be much earlier than the 19th century, but recalls Runton Wood, which probably stood on land long since washed away. In February 1605/6, surveyors acting for James I, as Duke of Lancaster, reported on all the woodland in the 'Manor of Beeston alias Beeston Regis iuxta Mare', which had recently been granted to Thomas Heriott and John Shelbury. Measured in the woodland manner at 18 feet to the pole rather than the normal 16½ feet, this consisted of 12 acres of small sapling oaks whose growth was 'greatlye hindered, with the salt water of the mayne Sea, Continually beatinge uppon the same grownde and hath eaten and consumed awaye parte of the grownde thereof'. Wood Point, as mentioned elsewhere, disappeared soon after World War 2.

Industry

Apart from the previously mentioned iron production on the heath near the 'Roman Camp', and perhaps near Incleborough Hill, there has been little industrial activity in Runton. Yet small-scale industrial processes have been carried out here, even though the evidence has largely disappeared or been removed.

Retting pits – for soaking the fibres of hemp or flax – are mentioned as being at the northern edge of West Runton Common in 16th century manor court rolls. There was also a reference in the 1490s to 'an holde lyme kill' at Marl Pit lands not far from Oxwell Cross. Within living memory there were the remains of another old lime kiln near the Old Butts close to Woman Hithe.

With lime being burnt to provide mortar, bricks also were made locally. Faden's map of 1797 shows a brickground on Brick Kiln Lane in East Runton, where the works were closed in April 1949 and demolished mid-1950. The squat conical kiln was of the brick-bar type and had a capacity of 38,000 bricks, producing in its time tiles and both white and red bricks. A similar kiln with a capacity of 32,000 bricks was operated at Oxwell Cross from 1904 to 1939. This also was demolished, in March 1951.

In about 1899, new Cromer Gas Works were built just inside the Runton boundary at a point convenient for a rail siding where coal could be brought in and by-products taken out. Rendered redundant by modern pipeline techniques, which first brought manufactured gas from Norwich and later natural gas from Bacton, even the gasholders – one only completed in the mid-1950s – have now gone.

What is probably the last traditional herring-house at Runton to retain its internal fixtures is situated on the Lower Common, but has long been used simply as an outhouse.

The only prominent industrial relic is the once-derelict tower mill at East Runton. While there are references to windmills in the Middle Ages, their sites are not precisely known, for wooden post-mills leave little trace when they decay. There is, however, at West Runton, the Mill Hill on which part of Kingswood Centre stands, but this seems to have been arable land at the end of the 15th century. At East Runton, Mill Hill is the one in the middle of the triangle formed by the railway embankments. No mill is shown on Faden's map, and the present tower is thought to date from the early 19th century. Last worked in about 1908, the mill had a cap of the Norfolk type which rather resembled a clinker-built boat with square bow and stern. The last remaining woodwork of this was removed shortly after the last World War on the grounds of safety. The mill has now entered a happier phase of its life. It

Runton mill in the late 19th century.

has been finely restored as an unusual home, now complete with cap, gallery and fantail, but without sails.

White's *Directory* of 1845 notes that East Runton was a fishing station. Whether one can term fishing an industry in the days of oar and sail is perhaps debatable, but it was undoubtedly a seasonal occupation. It is rare for actual occupations to be stated in most documents, but a few wills from the 15th and 16th centuries record bequests of fishing gear, e.g. manfares of nets such as twelve scores, flues (or flews), halvers and spirling nets. Most of these terms are now obsolete and of uncertain meaning, but twelve scores were probably for herring and spirling nets for sprats.

With boats depending on oars and sail, fishing was even more hazardous than today; as reminders about two of the writer's ancestors show. On 8th July 1870, Samuel Lawrence, aged 50, and his son Robert, aged 20, were both drowned off Cromer. At present it is not known what had happened, but it was ten days before Robert's body was found off Runton and two more before that of his father was recovered off Cromer. Such a fate was not uncommon among fishermen.

Alfred Leake and two of his sons were more fortunate. On 18th November 1893 a sudden storm, reminiscent of that on 31st January 1953, sprang up all over the country causing great damage. All the other Runton boats were able to return, though not without considerable risk, but Leake's large crab boat and one from Overstrand were in great difficulty and safe landing was impossible. At 3.30 p.m. the Cromer lifeboat with a crew of sixteen men under coxswain James Davies was launched. After about an hour the fishermen were with great difficulty pulled on board, but both boats were cast adrift. The lifeboat was brought ashore near the east breakwater at Cromer but in doing so shipped two heavy seas and five oars were broken. All were safely landed but the lifeboat suffered some damage. Meanwhile the tide still flowed two hours after the time of normal high water.

There are only a few fishing boats left at Runton now, but with petrol or diesel engines and powered capstans, they are able to go much further and to haul heavier loads than their predecessors.

Recent developments

Since the publication of the first edition of this booklet there have been several events of interest in the parish – one of international importance and others mainly of local concern. The first of these was the discovery and subsequent excavation of the West Runton elephant. In December 1990, following a stormy night, two local naturalists walking along the beach on the look-out for any fossils uncovered by the sea found protruding from the base of the cliff what proved to be the pelvis of a very large elephant. Further storms a year later uncovered more bones which were noted by another amateur. A small-scale excavation, mounted by the Norfolk Museums Service, recovered about a quarter of the skeleton of a large elephant estimated to have been about four metres in shoulder height and weighing about ten tonnes. Owing to the difficulty and danger of tunnelling into the cliff face a small flint wall was built to protect the remaining bones from erosion by the sea until a full-scale excavation could take place.

With major funding from the Heritage Lottery Fund and further donations from private and corporate bodies the Norfolk Archaeological Unit, working in partnership with a leading Swedish archaeological consultancy, began work early in October 1995. In order to expose a site approximately 15 by 5 metres it was necessary to remove 19 metres of overburden cut on three sides to an angle of 45 degrees for safety reasons. The removal of the fragile bones needed much plaster bandaging like that used to protect a broken limb; in the case of the skull a steel cage had to be constructed. The excavation took about nine weeks.

The elephant was a male about 40 years old, and died between 600,000 and

700,000 years ago. It is the best preserved ever to have been found and is 85% complete. The hope is that a full-sized replica and the bones may be put on display, possibly in the local neighbourhood, but as ever financial considerations may be a problem. The actual site, some 200 to 300 metres east of West Runton Gap (Woman Hithe), has been backfilled.

The Commons Enquiry of 1976 had left open the question of ownership of the commons, but the lord of the manor of Runton Hayes, Mr R. E. W. Batt, subsequently claimed that he was the owner of all the commons in Runton. Following an inquiry held at Cromer in November 1992, at which he was the sole claimant, he was indeed declared to be the owner of all these commons. Subsequently, without a further inquiry, it was found that the small common at Deer's Hill had been previously absorbed into the Golf Links.

Just before Christmas 1995, the shape of things to come was revealed when Town Hill and Incleborough Hill were sold to the National Trust. Since 1925 it has been technically illegal to drive a vehicle more than a few yards across a common. Following rumours of demands for payment for easement for vehicular access across the commons, owners of properties bordering commons received letters stating that a reasonable charge for such easements was 10% of the property value when sold. An Act of Parliament has subsequently reduced this figure to 0.25% or 2% in most cases, depending on the age of the property. This is still an ongoing problem.

Another event of importance, despite vociferous objections particularly from residents of Cromer, was the construction by Anglian Water of a sewage works on the site of the former Cromer Gas Works. As noted above this lies just inside the East Runton boundary.

Waste water from Overstrand, Cromer, East and West Runton, Beeston Regis and Sheringham is now pumped to the new treatment centre. The treated effluent is then pumped back to the site of the former brick works at Oxwell Cross and thence via a pipe laid below the beach and the seabed at Goss's Gap, rising in deep water to lie on the seabed. This outfall pipe is some two kilometres long and replaces the various short cast iron outfalls which so disfigured the wet sand. It is undoubtedly this new system that has enabled both Cromer and Sheringham to obtain Blue Flags for their beaches. At low water there is now a stretch of wet sand from Cromer to West Runton free of man-made obstructions. The beach, particularly at East Runton, is now a great attraction to surfers, who have erected on the cliff there a weather vane in memory of some of their fraternity who have died in the last few years.

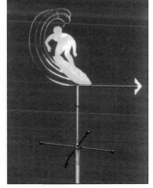

The wooden sea defences on the right are gradually succumbing to the waves; recent defence work has concentrated on the gaps at East and West Runton – granite blocks at East Runton and deflecting (page 2) and retaining walls here at West Runton.

Finally, mention must be made of coastline management that has taken place since late 2005 at West Runton, and still continues at the time of writing at East Runton. Both these schemes have attracted substantial grants from the Department for the Environment, Food and Rural Affairs (DEFRA). At West Runton, where beach levels continue to lower, access was no longer suitable for vehicles. A ramp has been provided to permit fishermen and the contractors of the North Norfolk District Council to have access for the foreseeable future. At East Runton, the long term plan, made more urgent by a major storm in March 2005, involves partial rebuilding of the sea wall, placing a flexible rock armour band and extending the ramp further into the beach. Public access is also being improved.

Conclusion

It is hoped that this amended and extended account of some of Runton's past may have been of interest, in spite of its lack of continuity. With luck, some of the gaps, whether due to ignorance, lack of material or any other reason, may be filled in by further work, for research into local history is a continuous process, albeit a very slow one. The writer acknowledges the invaluable assistance of John Creasey in making this revision; and the publisher would welcome further information and comments on, or corrections of, this effort.